Memories of Africa

Memories of Africa

Stories from a Pioneer Missionary

MARY SCHMELZENBACH

Nazarene Publishing House
Kansas City, Missouri

ISBN: 083-411-5077

Printed in the
United States of America

Cover Design: Royce Ratcliff

10 9 8 7 6 5 4 3 2 1

To our three children
Harmon Lee
Marilyn Joyce
Dennis Ray
who have blessed our home
with their presence and stood by
us so faithfully

Mary Schmelzenbach is a retired missionary who served 37 years with her husband, Elmer, in Swaziland and the Republic of South Africa for the Church of the Nazarene.

She received her degree in nursing from Northwest Nazarene College and responded to God's call to missionary service after hearing Louise Robinson (Chapman) speak at a nurses' meeting in Nampa, Idaho. While at NNC, she met Elmer Schmelzenbach, son of pioneer missionary Harmon Schmelzenbach. They were married in November 1934.

In 1936 the Schmelzenbachs were appointed as missionaries to Swaziland. During their career in Africa, Mary served as a nurse. Elmer taught in the Bible school and served as pastor, evangelist, field superintendent, and council chairman.

The Schmelzenbachs retired in September 1972. Elmer passed away in 1989. Mary resides in Bethany, Okla.

Contents

Introduction

This book is more than a dedication to my sister, Beula Palmer. She is seven years older than I am, but since our other brothers and sisters left home while I was still very young, Beula and I formed a close, loving relationship. She made a real impact on my life.

When Elmer and I went to "dark" Africa, as it was called then, we were stationed in remote areas. It was not easy to get the things we needed. This was before the days of box work and LINKS when local churches sent things to missionaries. Beula often came to my rescue with clothing for the children. I would send drawings of the children's feet and she would buy shoes one size larger and mail them to me. She sent numerous parcels of clothing and even toys. I know she spent many hours preparing the boxes for shipping. I can never repay her and will always be indebted to her.

When we retired, she gave me back all the letters I had written to her from Africa. The stories in this book come from those letters.

As you read about our life in Africa, remember I am talking about the early days there. Many conditions and facilities are very different now. This book will give you a realistic view of missions some 50 to 60 years ago.

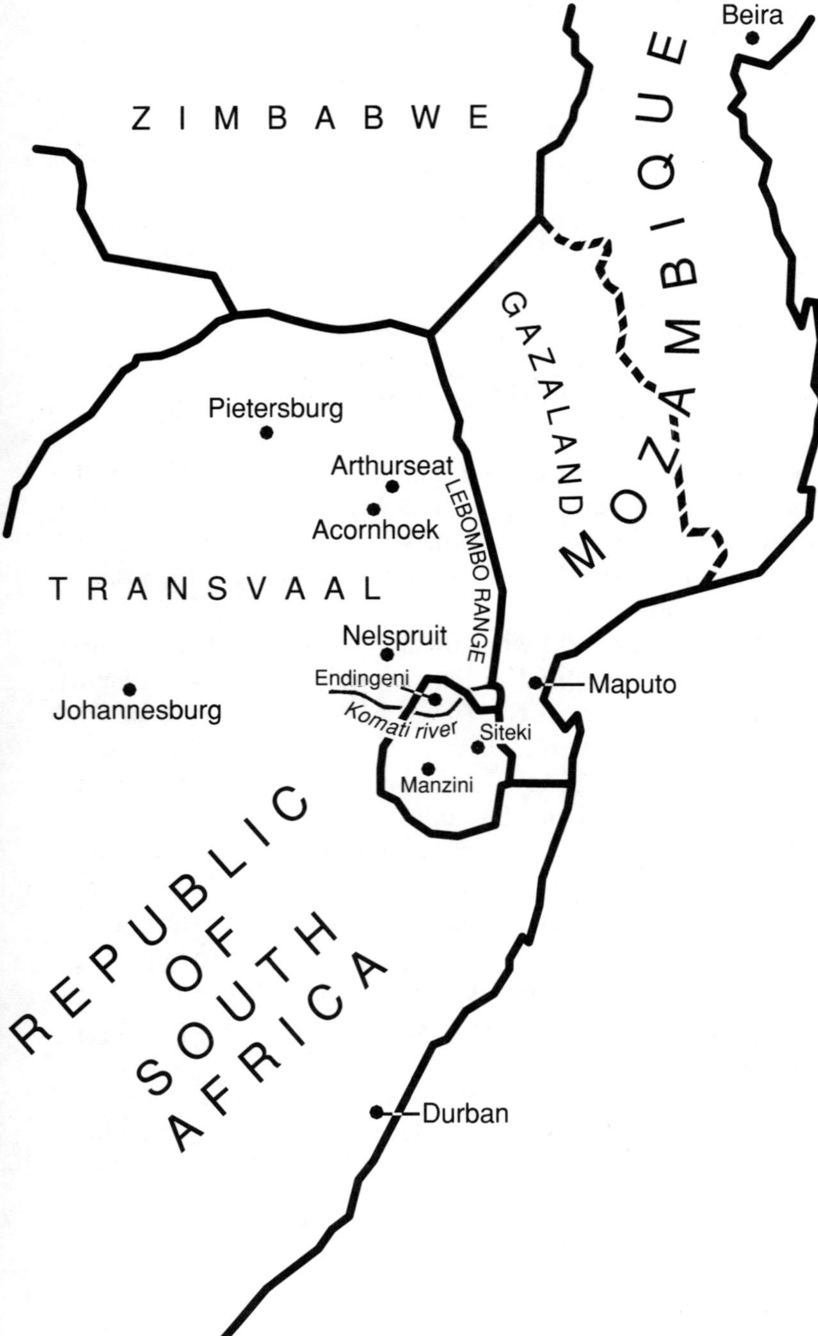

ZIMBABWE
MOZAMBIQUE
Beira
GAZALAND
Pietersburg
Arthurseat
Acornhoek
LEBOMBO RANGE
TRANSVAAL
Nelspruit
Endingeni
Komati river
Maputo
Johannesburg
Siteki
Manzini
REPUBLIC OF SOUTH AFRICA
Durban

1

Early Days

I was the ninth child born into the Snyder family. By the time I came along, my two older sisters and a brother had left home, but many stories that have been passed down in our family cause me to believe there was never a dull moment with nine children, all at home at the same time.

My father had one of the first cars in the country. The older brothers, the new generation, adapted quickly and usually drove the car. Dad, however, was more cautious. He built a small temporary shed to house the car. To get into this little building, it was necessary to drive up a small incline.

One day Dad ventured out for a drive. When he came home and started to drive into the shed, there were five sons hiding behind the wide-open doors. When Dad wasn't looking they sneaked behind the car and held it back. Dad stepped on the gas and finally plunged into the garage. By now, all five boys were pushing as hard as they could. Dad and the car went into garage and straight on through the other end of the little building. All five boys quickly hid and watched the results of their prank. Dad sat in the car for a while, talking to himself. The boys raced into the house and when Dad came in they asked him what happened. This was a favorite story repeated over and over again throughout the years. The boys would laugh so hard that tears would roll down their faces as they remembered the incident.

Another day, during the winter months, one of our horses, Old Flory, died. Dad told the boys to take her to the pasture, dig a grave, and bury her. Because the ground was frozen, digging was hard work. When the grave was deep enough for the body of the horse, the boys rolled her over into it. But the grave was so shallow that the horse's feet stuck straight up into the air. The boys carefully covered over Old Flory and returned home. What they didn't know was that Dad went out to inspect their work. He made them go out and dig a hole large enough to completely bury the horse.

Those were the horse-and-buggy days. We faithfully attended a little community church. Services were held at a schoolhouse a few miles from home. Mother, Father, and I would get in the buggy and start out. Our old white horse knew just where we were going. She would take us to the schoolhouse, go up to the hitching rack, and stop without ever being guided.

During my first year of school, one of my brothers was still taking some classes. I walked the two and a half miles each day with him, but I had to take two steps and then run two or three more to keep up with him. He was always telling me to hurry up. Later, going to school by myself was a nightmare to me. I was afraid to walk alone because of all the coyotes that ran wild through the fields.

I am thankful for the things that I learned from my parents. My mother, a very tiny woman, raised nine children. I do not think she ever had any of the conveniences of life. I remember that she washed our clothes on a washboard, used her own homemade soap, and carried the water to the house from an outside pump. She boiled clothes in a big boiler and hung them out on the line in freezing weather until the overalls and dresses were frozen stiff. She would then bring them in the house like a stack of firewood.

My mother was never too busy to help a neighbor. If there was a death in the family, she went to the home and helped. One time she even made cough medicine out of cactus for the country doctor.

During the dust bowl days in western Kansas, my parents decided to move to Idaho, where some of my brothers and a sister already lived. I entered Northwest Nazarene Academy and later went on to Northwest Nazarene College.

I met my husband, Elmer, at college. We found we had many things in common and our friendship grew. We both worked long hours at several jobs and tried to encourage each other. These times of ministering to each other deepened our friendship. We became engaged and Elmer convinced me that he needed me to go to Africa with him.

I decided to take some nurse's training along with my last year of college, and in 1933 I received a B.S. in nursing.

Elmer finished college before I did. He applied to the General Board for assignment to Africa. However, the country was in the midst of a deep depression, and there was no money to send any missionaries. The board suggested that Elmer pastor a church until there was money to send us. Since we were not married yet, Elmer went to Cle Elum, Wash., to pastor and I went back to the hospital to work and write my state board exams.

We were married in November 1934, and I went with my husband to the little church in Washington.

Since the General Board had told us it would be some time before we could go to Africa, we decided to start our family while we were still in the States. A son was born to us in December of the following year. We named him Harmon after his Grandfather Schmelzenbach who was a pioneer missionary to Africa. Can you guess what happened next?

When Harmon was one month old, we received a letter from Nazarene Headquarters in Kansas City saying, "You have been appointed to go to Africa as missionaries for the Church of the Nazarene. Can you go in four weeks?" We looked down into that basket at that tiny baby and wrote back, "Please give us six weeks." The board was understanding and agreed.

After saying good-bye to our dear Cle Elum church friends, we journeyed to Nampa, Idaho, to finish our final shopping, packing, and marking things for shipment to Africa.

Elmer and Mary Schmelzenbach, March 1936.

2

We're on Our Way

Early on the morning of my birthday, we left Nampa for New York. I think I can safely say that I am the only woman who has walked from Nampa to New York carrying a crying baby. Harmon had colic, and I was very aware of the unsympathetic frowns of the other train passengers who were not happy listening to the wails of a colicky baby. So I walked the train aisle with him or stayed in the tiny lavatory, trying to get him to sleep.

We arrived in New York at 2:30 P.M. on March 30. We found our ship and went aboard. At midnight the foghorn blew and the ship's visitors left. Ticker tape was thrown to shore and we slowly pulled out into the cold Atlantic. We arrived in England on April 11, after a wonderful trip on the ocean liner the *Berengaria.*

On Easter Sunday we attended church at Westminster Abbey. We took Harmon, our baby, with us. After the service, we enjoyed looking around. We saw name plates of many famous people who were buried there. Years later, as I related this experience to some of our British missionaries, they were astonished. They told us we had made a serious blunder. It seems as though back then only royalty was allowed to go to Westminster Abbey for services—and never with a child. They told us that attendance there was by invitation only. I must confess I wondered about the small crowd on Easter Sunday.

On April 17 we left London. We sailed through the Bay of Biscay. The water was very rough and everyone aboard was sick. Elmer was sure he was going to die. The bunks were so narrow that Elmer, a big man, couldn't lie on his back, and the coconut fiber mattresses had already been shaped to figures other than our own. Standing in the bathroom, which was over the propeller, I had to brace myself to keep from falling while I washed out a few baby clothes. We tied the baby's basket securely between our two bunks.

We passed volcanic Mount Stromboli, then through more straits between Italy and Sicily where it was very warm. Our first glimpse of Africa was at Tangier where we stopped for a few hours. We dropped anchor at Gibraltar, and a few hours later took a course north to the Isle of Palma and on to Marseilles, France, where we spent seven hours in port. We did a little sight-seeing and sailed at 8 P.M.

At Port Said, which is the entrance to the Suez Canal, we were swamped with people who wanted to sell curios, candy, flowers, cards, and artifacts. They wanted to rent us a carriage, perform magic, take our pictures, sell us stamps, or take us on a tour. They would put things in Harmon's little hands. When we had to take it away from him and give it back to the vendor, of course he would cry. We finally decided it was a losing battle and went back to the boat.

We left Port Said at one o'clock in the morning, but since we wanted to see the Suez Canal, we got up and went out on deck. On either side of the canal was desert. However, occasionally we would sail by an oasis where there were coconut palms, green vegetation, and people working with their camels and donkeys. The Suez Canal is 87½ miles long, and the passage time was 15 hours.

When we sailed through the Red Sea, we really got a chance to get warmed up. One day it was 140 degrees on deck. The captain stopped the boat and turned it toward a slight breeze, but it didn't help too much. Our captain pointed out spots of interest as we traveled, such as the places where the children of Israel were supposed to have camped and then where they crossed the Red Sea.

Our next stop was Aden, but it was so hot no one went ashore. Later on we crossed the Equator, and we all declared that we felt the bump as we went over it.

Mombasa, a slave trade port in earlier days, was where I first saw bananas and coconuts growing. We took a tour around the city. This was a welcome respite from such a long, confining trip. Many people disembarked at this port.

By now we were anxious to get to our destination. Six long weeks on the ocean, traveling with a baby, and trying to do laundry was difficult for me. Remember, there were no disposable diapers in those days. Toward the end of our trip, one of the sailors offered to do the laundry for me. From that time on, there were baby clothes flying in the breeze on a line strung between two huge smokestacks on the top deck. But, oh, the color of little Harmon's clothes. The smoke didn't help them either. I wondered if the Lord was preparing me for Africa.

Some days later we arrived in Beira, Mozambique, where we stayed two days; then on to the city of Lourenço Marques, where we left the ship at last. The night before we were to disembark we ran into a storm. Everyone went to bed early to try to avoid being seasick.

When we finally arrived in Lourenço Marques we stood on the deck watching the passengers hurry off the boat. We thought there was no need for us to be in a rush, for we did not expect anyone to be there to meet us. All of a sudden, we heard someone shout, "Elmer, hurry and get off. We have come to meet you." To our delight, three couples from the Stegi Mission were there to greet us. However, after discussing the situation, it was decided that we would spend the night aboard the ship since it was very late and we could not get through customs. Besides, if we stayed on board, we would have another night's free lodging.

The next morning, however, we were up early, packed,

and off the ship that had been our home for so long. We made it through customs and were on our way to Stegi, Swaziland, where we were to be stationed. How excited we were.

It was a cloudy, drizzly day, but as we finally turned into the gate at the mission station, the yard was full of people waiting to greet us. They each had branches of trees and ferns and were joyously waving them.

Elmer greeted the people in their own language. Even though he was raised in Africa, I thought that was pretty good since he had been away at school and in the States for 11 years. The people were very happy to see him return. The highlight of his return and welcome was to have Joseph, his father's right-hand man for many years, come into the yard on his bicycle. Joseph had ridden for about 80 miles, several days' journey, to get there. He took one look at our baby and said, "We have another missionary."

3

The Beginning Years
(1936-39)

We were taken on a tour of the station the next day by Rev. and Mrs. Carl Mischke and were introduced to our new responsibilities. Elmer would teach some classes in the Bible school and have charge of the work over the district. My assignment was the medical work. This included both the Africans and Europeans, since there was not a doctor near for the Europeans to consult for minor conditions. I was told that Dr. Hynd, from our Nazarene hospital at Bremersdorp, would visit the clinic once a month. It almost overwhelmed me when I thought about my assignment. There were new people, a new culture, a new language, and new diseases. I knew I would have to make many of my own medicines. In addition, I had a three-month-old baby and a home to care for. I was so thankful for a good national nurse who could take responsibility and even speak English. Most of all, I was grateful for a husband who knew and understood the people and their language and could help me with most of my difficulties.

Within a week after our arrival, we were at Endingeni, Elmer's old home station. Another great welcome awaited us. Elmer was to preach at the camp meeting. What an experience this was for us as we watched the church groups come over the hills all day long. Many would wait at the top of the hill above the station until everyone from their congregation had arrived. Then they would come in as a unit, singing at the top of their voices. Many were waving white flags and banners as they came. Their blankets and clothing were tied up in a roll that they carried on the top of their heads. Sometimes there was even a small cooking pot tied to the bundle. Their babies were on their backs. Bright head scarves and clothing made them a beautiful sight to see.

We gathered together that first night in a huge tabernacle that had been built at the site of the original Schmelzenbach home. Dry grass had been cut and spread on the floor for the people to sit on. As the building filled up, we stood and sang. Then the leader would invite the people to move forward. There were no seats to hinder their moving—only dry grass and dust. This activity was repeated several times until everyone was crowded in. Children sat around our feet and even on the front of the platform. Gas pressure lamps, hanging from the ceiling wires, lit up the building. All I could see was a great mass of people, and I wondered how I would ever learn to know them all.

Early in the service, a young woman sitting in front of me let out a blood-curdling scream that was terribly frightening to me. Hardly anyone paid any attention to her, but some of the girls got up and quickly led her outside. We were told later that she was a mental patient who often came to the station because people there were good to her and gave her food. These handicapped people are often ill-treated or neglected in their homes.

After a wonderful camp meeting, and visits with Elmer's old friends, we were ready to go back to our station and get started on our own work.

Kraal Visiting

We were told that if we wanted to be good missionaries, one of the first things we should do was to get out into the homes of the people, learn their customs, and make friends. So, after the heavy part of our work was done for the day, Elmer and I would get on horses and go out to the villages.

The Schmelzenbachs' first mode of transportation.

While visiting a kraal one day, we came to several donkeys and noticed that one was very lame. In fact, it could hardly walk. Then we noticed that someone had cut about an 18" square piece of skin from its hip. Elmer told me this was often done. The piece of skin was then taken to the witch doctor, who cooked it or ground it up and made medicine out of it. The witch doctor then sprinkled the medicine over the land when he doctored their gardens, so they would produce better crops. Elmer said his father taught many of the nationals to use fertilizer for the first time. They were very skeptical until they saw how much better the missionary's garden grew and the better crops it produced.

One day we went 10 or 15 miles by horseback to visit kraals. I was very tired when we got home. During our supper hour, a man rushed up to the door and knocked frantically. There had been a truck accident near one of the kraals, and he wanted us to come and help with the injured. At a big wedding and dance, the driver had drunk too much. As he drove home, he hit a telephone pole. Eight people riding with him were badly injured. One man had a compound fracture of the leg; another, two compound arm fractures. One man was tossed out on the gravel road and landed on his head. I could lift his scalp from his eyebrows back about six inches to the top of his head. We worked until about 2 A.M. giving first aid, easing their cries of pain, before the ambulance from Bremersdorp arrived. So ended my tiring day.

Laundry Woes

I am now sure that I was learning about wash day on the boat. Here at Stegi, water is very scarce. Our clothing has to be taken to the river on wash day by an African girl. Each piece is dipped into the water, laid on a huge rock, rubbed with strong soap, and scrubbed up and down on the rock by hand. It is then rinsed in the river and hung on the bushes to dry, as it is much too heavy to carry back to the station when wet. Many times a sock, or other piece, got away and floated on down the river. Talk about tattletale gray! The hot sun faded the colored clothes and, of course, with all the rubbing the clothes did not last very long. Now I know why the African children wear just a string of beads around their waists.

Chiggers and More Chiggers

A man came into the hospital complaining about his feet. He could hardly walk. We admitted him, for my African nurse knew exactly what was wrong. His feet were full of chiggers. These are not like the chiggers you have in the States. These burrow under the skin and grow, forming a little sack around them, about the size of a small pea. The method the Africans use in removing them is to take a dull safety pin and gradually work the skin away from the little sack until they can remove the insect intact. They worked for days on this man's problem and finally removed over 200 chiggers from his feet. He was so happy that he could walk again.

Floods and Bad Weather

The rivers overflow their banks quickly when it rains hard and long. We heard recently that over 100 people lost their lives at the mouth of the Komati River. One man said he saw seven large snakes in one tree—two mambas, two cobras, a huge python, and two others he did not recognize. Everything that could climb was in trees. This included red fire ants. The ants attacked the people until they almost went mad fighting the stinging ants. Many of the people jumped out of the trees into the water to escape the ants, only to be washed away in the floods. I'm glad we live on the top of the Lobombo Range.

Because of the floods, malaria will be bad this year.

Baby Noises

I awakened Elmer. "Listen," I said. "I thought I heard a baby crying."

"No," said Elmer, "it is not a human baby but a bush baby. It is a little soft, furry animal about the size of a squirrel. It cries just like a baby, but starts and stops more often."

Council Time

Council time means days of excitement and planning. Sometimes missionaries live for a year with only the visit of a few other missionaries, or we work with just a few others in isolated places. Can you imagine how we all like to come together for fellowship?

Our first council meeting was held in Dr. Hynd's house. As we got down on our knees to pray, I saw a big, odd-looking insect in the shag rug Mrs. Hynd had on the floor in front of the fireplace where Rev. Penn, Sr., and I were to kneel. As I got down, I tried to step on it. Mr. Penn was already kneeling, and it shot over to him and went up his trouser leg. Not realizing the danger, I waited until the meeting was over, then I told Elmer about what had happened. He asked me what it looked like, and when I described it, he knew immediately that it was a scorpion. Elmer told Brother Penn, who immediately hurried off to his room. He found the scorpion nestled in the folds of his trousers but was spared a bad sting. I certainly never took insects for granted again.

May 1937

On the occasion of the coronation of their Majesties King George VI and Queen Elizabeth of England on May 12, 1937, the people of Stegi presented me with a medallion of honor. They also gave me a letter in "Appreciation of her excellence and kindly services." I was humbled to be so honored.

A Wonderful Gift from Home

A friend of ours in Ohio sent us $200 to be used for something we needed. You will never guess what we bought. We went to Lourenço Marques and bought a refrigerator. There is only one among all the missionaries, and it is not on our station. The refrigerator has three burners under the freezing unit, like an oil stove. Each night we have to pull out the burner unit, pour one bottle of kerosene in the tank, and light the burners. When the oil is gone it begins to freeze.

We have to do this daily, but we don't mind. It is wonderful to have something cold, and a real blessing when someone is sick with a fever. However, our main problem had been keeping food from spoiling. We buy milk from a neighbor who knows nothing about cleanliness. This means that we have to carefully strain the milk and boil it before we can use it. We boil it again in the evening to make sure it stays sweet until the next morning.

I made ice cream and one day when Joseph was here, I gave him a dish of ice cream. He knew what pudding was and thought this was pudding. He took a big spoonful and was surprised. He put his hand over his mouth and mumbled, "It burns! It burns!" The Africans have no word for ice. All they have seen is hail, and they call that rocks or stones.

A Trip to an Outstation

Recently Elmer found and bought an old two-wheeled cart. We hitched our mule, and one borrowed from a neighbor, to the cart and we were ready to make a trip to an outstation. Elmer usually goes on horseback, so I cannot go with him, but with the cart I decided to try it.

The church is only 17 miles away, but I found out that 17 miles in a two-wheeled cart pulled by two mules is a long trip. Late that afternoon, about halfway home, we met a car. It was the Carl Mischkes who had come to meet us. They rightly guessed that I would have had enough of the mule cart by that time. I was glad to ride in their car the rest of the way home.

Water Shortage

Water is a very precious commodity in the outstations and sometimes very scarce. The people walk miles to get it and then carry it home on their heads. Here, we treat water with respect.

When you see the color of the water, you do not wonder why we never drink it before first boiling it. When we are at the outstations, we wait to be served tea because we know the water has been boiled. Missionaries have been known to brush their teeth, shave, and even fill hot water bottles with tea. This conserves precious water that has already been used.

Minor Surgery

Little did I realize, when I went to Africa, that I would not only be a nurse but a veterinarian. Early one morning, someone came to our door and told Elmer that our hogs had gotten out of their pen during the night. They had been in a fight with our neighbor's hogs. Our pigs were all cut up in the fight, some with gashes as deep as the width of my hand. After Elmer examined them, he said to me, "Mary, I have told the Bible school boys to get in the pen and hold the hogs so you can sew them up. I have to leave for an outstation now, or I will not be there in time for the service."

I stood there in bewilderment. What kind of sutures do you use on a pig? I didn't think I had anything heavy enough, but finally decided to use some ordinary string. I boiled the string, and all morning, while the students held the squealers, I sewed up eight hogs. I put iodoform on the wounds to keep the flies away, and in no time the cuts healed nicely. Since the sutures were not the kind that dissolve, I often wondered just how much string the Bible school students had in their bacon later on.

Uncertain Death

One of our pastors, far out on the district, sent us word that his little daughter had died of malaria. He wanted us to please come and have the funeral.

We went to the home, and as the men were busy digging the little grave, we tried to comfort the grieving parents. When it was time to prepare the body for burial, we started to wrap the child in her blanket and sleeping mat, as was the custom. As I looked down at her, I saw a slight flicker from her eyelids. On closer examination, I found that she was not dead, but very sick from cerebral malaria. We took her to the hospital and it was not long before she was up and well again. How close we came to burying the child alive. This may have been done many time by the Africans, as same-day burial does not give much time for close observation. This was a great lesson to me in my early missionary work.

Depression Years

During those difficult years, our preachers got very small salaries. Their money could buy about one big sack of cornmeal each month. This did not go very far when they had big families to feed. Their meals were nothing but a big dish of porridge, with a little coarse brown sugar on it for breakfast at midmorning, and another dish of porridge, cooked stiff, in the evening. With the evening meal they picked a kind of weed, cooked it, and made a gravy to eat with their porridge. If they can raise a garden of a few peanuts, sweet potatoes, or pumpkins, they are well-off.

God Provides

At quarterly meeting time, when it was time for reports, Pastor Jerioti jumped to his feet. He reported that he had been having a hard time feeding his family on his small salary, but that God had provided an unusual way for him to make some money.

He remembered an article he had read in a paper about a company in Durban that wanted snakeskin to make into shoes, purses, and watch straps. He found out that this company would pay so much per foot to anyone who could send them a cured skin.

One day, while visiting his people, he came across a very large python. Jerioti quickly killed the snake with his knob-kerry (club) and skinned it. After curing it, he sent it to Durban to the factory. In a few weeks, he received a nice check. This helped him feed his family. He ended his report by saying, "Elijah was fed by ravens, but snakes help to feed us."

Dispensary Duty

Much of my time is spent in the dispensary making ointments for burns and scabies—tonics, diuretics, cough syrup, and many other types of medicines. One day I discovered that the young men in the school were finishing the cough medicine much too fast. On quietly inquiring about it, I found they liked the sugar in it and were pouring it on their porridge for breakfast. I didn't say anything, but I put some quinine in the next batch, for they all had malaria, and from then on, the medicine lasted longer.

I am continually exposed to so many things. I often wonder just how long it will be before I take something home to Harmon. Diphtheria, measles, whooping cough, tuberculosis, scabies, leprosy, anthrax, and other things too numerous to mention are brought to me every day. After I prayed about it, I decided that was all part of the unknown bundle I left on the altar back in the States. It is hard to control some of these diseases because the wild animals also carry and spread them. African children do not get their shots like the children in the States, so some disease is always going around.

Help at Home

Since so much of my time is taken up at the dispensary, or out on calls, I needed help in my home. Many girls came and asked for work as they like to earn a little money to buy clothes or go to school. I had one girl to care for our bedroom and watch the baby. Small children are never allowed out to play without a girl to watch them. It is too dangerous because of the snakes. So, I hired another girl to help in the kitchen.

One morning, after she had been with us for a few weeks, I made pancakes for breakfast. After we sat down at the table in the dining room, I discovered we did not have syrup on the table. I asked the girl to bring the tin of syrup and described it to her. I also told her where she would find it. She was gone a long time and finally came in with a tin of varnish, which she had found on top of the cupboard. Thank goodness we discovered the mistake before we poured it on our pancakes.

But it isn't only the household help that makes mistakes. Recently I had guests and made a pot of coffee to serve them. Not until they had drunk their coffee and left did I discover that I had boiled a tarantula spider in the coffee. I was sure we would all be sick, but no one was. That episode was a well-kept secret for many years. After that, I not only looked in my shoes before I put them on but also looked in my pots and pans before cooking in them, and taught my kitchen girl to do the same.

Our First Home in Africa

We have been very busy, and there have been so many interesting things for me to see and do since our arrival that I haven't told you about our home.

We have just built a new dispensary here, and we have been given the old dispensary building as our home. A single

Elmer with his first car in Swaziland

lady had lived in it previously, and every time she needed more room for storage she put up another partition. Elmer is a big man and some of these halls and rooms were just too small for him. He began knocking out the extra partitions. Since it was an old building and the termites had eaten much of it away, the floor in the dining room parted company with the wall every time Elmer walked across the floor. Many creepy-crawly things came into the house through that opening as well.

Our furniture was old and had been used before. Our bed was only a three-quarter bed in size. The springs had long ago given out, and someone had put slats under them. Occasionally, in the middle of the night, one of the slats would let go and down to the floor we would go. We finally ordered a metal bed from Montgomery Ward. We paid $50.00 for it.

Our superintendent sent us a table and chairs that he bought for us in Johannesburg. Our cupboards were double orange crates stacked, with a curtain on the front. In the bedroom, we stacked orange boxes in two stacks and put a bar between them so we could hang up our clothes. Orange crates also served as bookcases.

Mosquitoes

In your last letter, Beula, you asked if we were well protected from mosquitoes. We always sleep under netting. We had one over our bed and another over the baby's bed with edges tucked under the mattresses. In the night, when I would have to get up to care for the baby, both nets would be loosened from the beds and invariably we would have a mosquito in bed with us. So I took the two nets that hanged from the ceiling, opened them, and sewed them together to make one large net and let them hang clear to the floor instead of being tucked under our mattresses. This solved the problem and also kept anything from crawling up the bedstead from the floor. We often see tarantulas crawling on the ceiling.

Recently, I sat down on a little throw rug in the bedroom to clean my white shoes before going on duty. From the corner of my eye, I saw a movement about three feet from me, next to the wall. On closer inspection, I discovered a snake. It didn't take me long to get out of there.

Yesterday Elmer put his hand down in a wastepaper basket to retrieve a paper he had discarded and came out with a tarantula hanging on to his finger. I grabbed a razor blade, lanced the bite area, soaked his hand in permanganate solution, and he felt none the worse for it. Tarantulas are usually not deadly, but occasionally someone dies from a bite. So, you see, we could be more mosquito and bug proof.

Bible School Students See the Ocean

When we told our Bible school students that we were on a boat for seven weeks when we came to Africa, it was almost more than they could comprehend. So we took five of them to Lourenço Marques to see the ocean. We took them aboard a big boat to look around. They were amazed.

We bought each of the five men a loaf of bread and some tinned beef along with 200 tiny bananas. You should have seen them enjoy that meal. We had a few bananas left when we got to the border between Mozambique and Swaziland. Because of health restrictions, they couldn't bring the bananas across the border. You should have seen the students stuff themselves instead of leaving those bananas behind. I was sure they would all be sick, but they survived.

An Unusual Case

I was called out on an unusual delivery. When I got to the hut the woman was already dead from hemorrhaging. The baby had been born but was still attached to the placenta. I did not know how long the mother had been dead or what damage had been done to the baby. I didn't know what else to do except tie the cord and take the baby back to the dispensary. No one in her family wanted her. The father said he did not have food for her nor a cow to supply milk. He said I could have her. We gave her the name of Alice. I found out later that this action is a method the people sometimes used to get someone else to raise their baby. Then when the child is old enough for the father to sell for a dowry, the parents want the child back.

It's Locust Time

This morning I saw my first locusts. A thick, black cloud of them passed over our house about 10 A.M. They swarmed around until almost 3 P.M. We all turned out with sticks and pans to bang on and made as much noise as we could to try to frighten them away from the orange blossoms and the garden. We were not able to save one of our gardens, which was quite a distance from the house. They ate everything.

The Nurse Becomes a Patient

Once in a while the missionary takes a turn at being the patient. I had some kind of spasm that doubled me over with pain. Medication didn't seem to help too much. Finally Elmer persuaded me to go to Bremersdorp to the doctor. As often happens, on the way to the doctor, I began to feel better. I can't imagine what hit me, but it was bad while it lasted.

Witchcraft Is Still at Work

Last Sunday was the closing service of our revival. We all

felt so sorry for a woman who came to the altar. Everything about getting saved was so new to her. When she finished praying, she told us that she had been sold to a man when she was a very little girl, and when she was old enough, she was sent to live with him. After their second child was born, her husband died. As is the custom, she was sent to live with her late husband's brother. Soon her two children died and later her brother-in-law's first wife also passed away. It seemed that everywhere she went, death followed her. Now she was accused of being the one who had bewitched her relatives and caused their deaths. Witchcraft is outlawed, but nevertheless, it is still practiced. The woman was just waiting to be killed and was very frightened. We felt powerless to help her except to encourage her to remain true to the Lord.

Busy Days

This has been an unusually busy month. Sybil, my nurse, has been on vacation. Alone, I have treated 400 patients, had 7 inpatients, 1 delivery, in addition to cooking and caring for my family. In my spare time, I have studied Zulu.

I have had so many men come to the dispensary who have been hit on the head as the result of their beer drinks. They usually wait until the wound is badly infected before they come to me.

One man was hit on the head with a pick. The wound was so deep his brain was exposed. The doctor wanted to operate, but the man refused. Later, he was seen working. He had taken a small baking powder can, fastened strings on it and tied it on his head, like a bonnet, to protect the hole from the flies that bothered him.

The men fight with their clubs and spears, but the women have only their teeth. They use them with stunning effect. They come to the dispensary with their fingers badly bitten, or a nose, ear lobes, and even pieces of their lips gone. Usually the witch doctor has treated them first. They worsen and finally come to see me.

The missionary or our Swazi preacher has a service with

them while they wait to be treated. Often they will start coming to church.

Customs

I am gradually learning some of the African customs. The day school is almost a block from us, but I can hear the children as they learn their lessons. They can learn English better if they speak it aloud. Just now they are learning "Twinkle, Twinkle, Little Star." They repeat it in unison, over and over, until they learn it.

All African children have their ears pierced. It is not just the size of a needle but quite a good-sized cut. Then a little piece of bamboo is inserted in the hole until it heals. They decorate themselves by hanging a bead or sometimes a safety pin in the hole. Don't laugh. Safety pins are very valuable and often are used as an engagement present. Most of our school children come from Christian homes, so they don't decorate much, but they have found that the holes in their ears are good places to carry or store their pencils.

We Have Twins

We have twin baby boys at the dispensary now. The mother requested us to name her babies, so we call them Peter and Paul. We had a hard time convincing the mother that she should keep both babies. Twins are not readily accepted in the African culture, but she has agreed to keep them.

Babies are tied to the mother's back while she works. This is fine in the daytime, but when night comes it is often a little chilly. Then the mother puts the babies in bed with her, under her blanket, even covering their heads. As a result, we get many burn cases. The only heat in the hut is a small, smoldering fire in the center of the hut. In cold weather they put their sleeping mat as close to the fire as possible. Often the baby rolls out from under the blanket and into the hot coals.

More Snake Stories

A little girl was brought to the dispensary yesterday who

had been bitten by a puff adder. I lanced the bite, treated her foot, and gave her an injection of snake-bite serum. Today her foot is badly swollen, but I believe she will be all right in time. When an adder bites, the flesh all falls away, leaving tendons exposed and deep holes. The wound takes weeks to heal and many times requires skin grafting.

Last week Elmer was walking along a little footpath when a cobra struck at him. Its fangs got caught in his trouser leg. He kept pulling at it in order to milk out as much venom as possible in case it took another strike at him. Finally the snake let go and was ready to strike again, but Elmer got away in time.

He came home holding the trouser leg away from him in case he had a scratch or sore on his leg that the poison could get into. I poured hot water over the spot. It turned the water milky, but there was no puncture and Elmer will be all right. We thank God, once again, for His protection.

Church Building Construction

Most of our outstation churches are very primitive. Mud walls are whitewashed inside and out. Some do not even have windows, just holes in the walls to let in light and ventilation. The churches may not have windows, but one thing they all have is an altar. It will be just a log split down the middle, with the flat side up and four small branches fit into it for legs.

Our churches have no benches for the congregation. Everyone brings a small mat or animal skin to sit on. For a visitor, the pastor will bring a chair from his home, one that he has probably made. There is usually one bench for the preachers to sit on. A little home-made table serves as a pulpit.

The termites love these buildings. They tunnel right through the mud and in no time they are in the grass-thatched roof. That means that it is necessary to rebuild our churches every few years. How we long for more money to replace these buildings with something more substantial.

Offering Time

Regardless of the building, the services are very interesting and rewarding. This morning it was offering time when the people brought their tithe of the yearly crop. Each one brought a tithe that represented how the Lord had blessed him down through the year.

Our leader brought an ox. Since he could not bring the animal into the church, he brought some hair from its tail, letting the people know he had an ox to give. Each woman brought her basket in on her head. The baskets were full of millet, sweet potatoes, peanuts, bags of corn, and feathers denoting chickens they had at home to give.

Occasionally someone brings a live chicken, with its legs tied together, and places it down at the front of the church. What they fail to remember is that the chicken could still flap its wings and try to fly. This causes quite a commotion during services until someone catches the chicken and carries it outside.

Eggs are always brought to this offering service. Sometimes they are eggs that have been found in a hidden nest and are about ready to hatch.

These services are always a good time to teach our new converts and the children that what we have comes from the Lord and that part of it should be given back to Him for His work.

African Names

The Africans usually give us all an African name. After they know us for a while, they come up with a name that describes some of our characteristics. Sometimes we hear these names, but more often the people keep them to themselves and only use them when they talk with each other in private. As far as I know, the only name I ever got was "Mother of Harmon."

Elmer's name was "Red Rooster," as he liked to fight with the boys with their sticks when he was growing up in

Africa. When we went back as missionaries, they refined his name to "Vusa Igama," which means "to resurrect his father's name."

An Unexpected Delivery

Did you ever take a bath in a little galvanized tub? That's all we have here. One night while I was doubled up in the tub, Elmer pounded on the door and called, "A hurry-up call for the nurse."

Quickly I climbed out of the tub, dried off, dressed, and went out. There in the car was a European patient with a new baby that had been born on the way to the dispensary. I finished the delivery there in the car and fixed a bed for her in the dispensary. I expected her to leave in 3 days, but to my surprise, she wanted to stay 10 days. She said she was very tired.

Under normal circumstances, I wouldn't have cared, although we are not really equipped to keep anyone that long, but I had no help at that time. Elmer and our cook had just left for the quarterly meeting at Endingeni. I had my housework, cooking, and other patients to care for. On top of it all, Harmon became very ill with a temperature of 104.2. He fussed continually, so I could not get a good night's sleep. I was surely glad when Elmer and the others returned to help.

More and more we have urged our African women to come to the dispensary to have their babies. It didn't take me long to discover just what kind of care they get in the kraal.

For a delivery, all the grandmothers in the area come in to give advice and help. The little mother is not allowed to make one cry or groan or they begin slapping her for not being a woman able to bear her pain. If she is in labor for a long time, a sharp piece of broken bottle comes in handy. There are many other treatments that are not healthy for the mother or the baby.

One very small woman came to see me while she was pregnant. We helped her as much as we could during the nine months. I had told her that she needed the skill of a doctor to have her baby, and that she must go to the government hospital. One day I missed her at the clinic and asked about her. The other women told me she had died. Her grandmother would not give permission for her to go to the hospital and while she was in labor, she had been horribly mutilated until both she and her baby died.

Swazi Decorations

When the Swazi women marry, they start wearing a skin skirt made from cowskin. They wear them day and night, even until the hair is worn off the hide. They get a new one about every five years.

Also when she marries, a Swazi woman begins to wear her hair on top of her head. She arranges it like a beehive and secures it with string and mud on the inside. She does not intend to ever take it down, although sometimes it has to be repaired. She usually has a hairpin, about eight inches long, stuck in her hair. When there is an uncontrollable itch inside her hair, it is scratched with the hairpin. On this hairpin, the woman will hang a few beads for an ornament. If she doesn't have a hairpin, she often uses a spoke from a bicycle wheel.

God Answers Prayer

Harmon has developed asthma since we have lived here at Stegi. Several times he has had spells that have really frightened us. I have not been trained to care for a child with asthma, so when he chokes and begins wheezing, we don't lose any time in heading for the hospital and a doctor's care.

Recently he had a very bad spell. We bundled him up and sped toward Bremersdorp. When we got to the hospital, Dr. Hynd rushed off to get an injection for Harmon. Between gasps for breath and wheezing, Harmon looked up at Elmer and me from his little cot and said, "Mommy, couldn't Jesus make me well?"

We agreed that Jesus could heal him, so we decided to ask Him about it. We prayed, and before Dr. Hynd could get back with the injection, Harmon had stopped wheezing and was breathing easier. We do not think the doctor ever had to give Harmon that injection. But we do know that from that day on, he has never had another bout with asthma.

"And a little child shall lead them" (Isa. 11:6). We were reminded of this many times through the years when we needed a lesson on faith and trust in God. Without His help, we would have failed many times during our missionary career.

4

Bremersdorp

(1939-42)

Transferred to Bremersdorp

Because the work here at Stegi is heavy, and because we are expecting a new baby soon, it seemed best to place another nurse here and move us to Bremersdorp where I would help in the hospital work and Elmer would take over the district work. I moved first, as it was nearly time for our baby to arrive, and if I waited too long the roads would be in terrible condition during the rainy season. I don't think this country has ordinary rains. They seem more like cloudbursts to me.

Marilyn Joyce arrived March 2, 1939. We are so thrilled. We now have a boy and a girl. I had a rough time for a few days, with a temperature of 105 degrees. I was glad when Dr. Hynd returned from Endingeni and started me on the road to recovery.

Back to Work

Ten days after Marilyn was born I was back on duty. I gave 35 intravenous injections and took 21 blood tests the first day. All patients are seen here in the clinic first. We care for those we can, and the doctor sees the rest. If necessary, he admits them to the hospital. I also have charge of the operating theater and scrub for all operations. That means I am on call day and night.

It is hard to leave a new baby at home all day, but

Elmer's mother is with us and Elmer is also at home. He is building a new room on our house for his mother. I work from 9:00 in the morning until 5:00 in the afternoon with an hour off for lunch when I can go home.

A woman in the hospital has just given birth to triplets. She is very unhappy. Her people say she must not keep them, as they are animals. No woman could have three babies; only animals have multiple births. We worked with her during her stay in the hospital and convinced her to keep her babies. She promised she would, but we do not know what happened when she got home.

When twins are born, the first is considered a human being and the second one is given to the grandmother who neglects it until it dies. Sometimes they just put the second baby in a clay pot and set it down by the river. Another of our patients has just had twins. She is begging us to keep one as she knows if she takes them both home, the second one will die of neglect.

Outstation Work

Elmer and Rev. Savage went to an outstation by horseback last week. They saw lion tracks in the mud beside the road on their way to the station. On the way back, there was a fresh kill in the middle of the road. They hurried on, and then spotted some Cape buffalo a short distance away. They really hurried then, for they were afraid they might be charged. The pastor later told them that a buffalo had recently charged two men. One of the men dove into a thornbush to get away. The other man was tossed between two thornbushes by the animal. Both men were badly injured. Elmer brought some of the thorns home. They measured eight and one-half inches long! I can't imagine what it would be like to land on one of those.

Rain—Too Much and Too Little

We had a heavy rain yesterday. Our house leaked like a sieve. The wind blew the rain under the tile roof and under the doors until our house was flooded. Our walls are streaked, and we had to take down some pictures as the mud plaster got wet and the pictures fell.

In Mozambique they have had a terrible drought. Many have died. The people have been eating mulberry leaves, roots, and grass, cooking them a little first to make them soft.

We just heard about a woman with five children who were starving. The mother decided to go to town and try to find some work so she could buy some food for her family. In town, no one would hire her because she had a small baby on her back. Finally, in desperation, she went to the edge of town and threw her baby into a big lake. Then she went back to town thinking she would get work. The police found out about it and put her in jail. Her four children are now home alone, and still hungry.

Calves and Gardens Don't Mix

Yesterday I had a beautiful vegetable garden, but last night the calves got into it and ate all my beans and lettuce. I also had some cantaloupe. They were the only ones I had seen since coming to Africa. Each day I would go out and look at them to see how much they had grown and figure how much longer I would have to wait to pick them. Yesterday my young gardener picked the melons. They were only about the size of baseballs. He brought them to me and said, "I think these are ready to cook." I almost cried. Sometimes one can't win.

Revival Time in the Outstations

Elmer has just finished a series of revival meetings in all the outstations. He says they are the best meetings he has had since he has been back.

At one of the services, while praying at the altar, Elmer heard a terrible commotion at the back of the church. It was a heathen woman with the most agonized look on her face. One of the pastors went back and led her to the altar. The men prayed with her, but she couldn't seem to get through.

Then Elmer asked if she had demon things at home. She said she did. The men told her to go home and get them and bring them to the church. She brought them to the church, piled them all outside, and asked the men to burn them. She brought a little mat that she shook the bones on, a little spear to kill the witch, bottles, beads, skins, medicine, and all that goes with demon worship. After the burning and a terrible struggle, the demons left her. She jumped to her feet and testified to the saving power of Jesus and deliverance from the demons.

A General Superintendent Visits

We surely have enjoyed the visit of General Superintendent Dr. J. G. Morrison. He ordained Elmer and Rev. Glen Grose at our council meeting. He also ordained our first national preachers. He delivered his famous sermon, "Three Loaves of Bread," for us.

Charles Jenkins, Dr. J. G. Morrison, and Elmer Schmelzenbach, 1939

Time for School

Harmon is now old enough to go to school, but since that is impossible, I am going to teach him at home. I have ordered the Calvert course so that I can start teaching him. I don't know how I can work it into my schedule, but I will have to try.

Surgery Plans Change Quickly

Yesterday a man came to the hospital who needed some minor surgery. The doctor told me to prepare for it today. Since it was minor, it would only take the two of us. I prepared the instruments on a tray. We put the man on the operating table. I started to give him the anesthetic when he suddenly sat up, jumped off the table, and took off running. He ran out the hospital door, down over the hill toward town as fast as he could go. His white hospital gown was flying behind him in the breeze. We stood and watched for a time, had a good laugh, and sent an ambulance to bring him back. The second attempt at surgery was successful.

Elmer Practices First Aid

It was revival time at Manzana. As usual, Elmer took several of the national pastors with him in the car.

After they left the main road, they followed little footpaths through the grass. The car hit a hidden stump that punched a hole in the oil pan. This meant they would have to walk the rest of the way and carry their provisions.

Although the national pastors had shoes, they had removed them to move faster and also keep the shoes nicer for church. One of the pastors stubbed his toe on a stone and tore the nail completely off. Elmer quickly found his first aid kit, applied medicine and bandages, and fixed Azariah up.

When they reached Manzana, they discovered that the pastor had killed a cow that day so there would be plenty of meat for the people to eat. Beef quarters were hanging up in the small grass hut where Elmer and the men were supposed to sleep.

Different sounds began to rise from each sleeper. Some of the men snored. Azariah's toe hurt so much he could not stand to have his blanket touch it. Soon the village dog smelled the meat and went into the hut. Azariah saw it and yelled at the dog to scare it away. The dog ran, but Azariah was afraid that dog would come back, so he carefully took his belt to use as a weapon in case the dog returned.

Later, waking up quickly after dreaming he had seen the dog again, Azariah grabbed his belt and came down hard with his buckle on what he thought was the animal—hitting his big white, bandaged toe. He raised up with a loud roar that awakened everyone. The men wanted to laugh, but they could see that Azariah was really suffering, so they sympathized with him instead.

After that meeting was over, Elmer got some oxen to pull his damaged car to a little trading store. He bought some soft, blue laundry soap and patched up the hole in the oil pan. He filled it with oil and drove home safely. They had a good revival in spite of all the difficulties.

An Unwelcome Visitor

Just as we were preparing to go to church last Sunday, I looked out in the yard and saw a cobra. With two small children playing out there each day, I didn't think I should let it get away. Everyone but the two children and I had already gone to church. With not a soul in sight to help me, I grabbed a long-handled hoe and went after it. Soon two small children and their pet cat were beside me. I chased the cat away and then chopped down hard on the snake with the hoe and cut off a few inches of its tail. That really made the cobra mad. He spread his hood and turned for me. I came down again with the hoe and managed to pin the snake to the ground.

There I stood, afraid to lift the hoe. Finally, after what seemed like a very long time, a man cut across the mission station toward the road. I called to him for help. How thankful I was to have him finish off that snake for me. Someone else can kill snakes from now on.

Harmon's Pet Chicken

Someone gave Harmon a baby chick as a pet. It didn't

last long, and when it died he was devastated. He decided that the best thing he could do was to give it a good burial. He fixed up a little box, got some flowers ready, and prepared to bury the chicken. He was the preacher, and Marilyn was the congregation. He dug a grave in the garden. They sang some choruses, and Harmon began to preach. (Elmer and I were hidden in the bushes watching and listening.)

Something in Harmon's sermon struck Marilyn funny and she began to laugh. He stopped preaching and gave her a good lecture about not laughing at a funeral. Then he finished his sermon and buried the chicken. Elmer and I wondered if he would be a preacher someday. Time will tell.

War Is Declared

War has been declared and our mail is not getting through. Very few letters have been received, but today we had a windfall. Twenty-six letters came from the States in one delivery.

Miss Fox had already left for her furlough when we got word that no other nurse could be sent to take her place at this time. Dr. Hynd wired her at the coast where she was waiting for her boat, and asked her to return to the field. What a disappointment that would be—to start one's furlough and then be called back. But she is returning.

Many Swazi men are being trained here in Bremersdorp to go north and help in the war effort. As a chaplain, they chose Rev. Samuel Dlamini to go with them. They will be sent north soon. Rev. Dlamini, dressed so nicely in his uniform, came to our door to tell us good-bye. After a cup of tea and a prayer, he was gone. He seemed anxious to be of service to God and his country.

Our First Real Holiday

For a little rest, we went to Gazaland and helped in two camp meetings. It was hot in the tent during service. I was amazed to see men stationed by the big tent poles, each with a long bamboo pole. Their job was to awaken the sleepers and also to urge mothers with crying babies to leave the service.

From Gazaland we went to the beach. The Jenkinses joined us here, and we went to the Game Reserve. We saw lions, hippos, warthogs, hyenas, giraffes, impala, waterbuck, kudu, zebra, jackals, wildebeests, monkeys, baboons, wild guinea fowl, and others. We didn't stay too long, for both Marilyn and Elmer were not feeling well. It is hard to camp and fix things for sick people.

Furlough Canceled

Because of the war, our furlough has also been canceled. We think we will go to Johannesburg for a little while.

While in Johannesburg, we bought the record of "God Bless America." You should hear Harmon and Marilyn singing it at the tops of their voices while in bed at night.

It's Christmas

The missionaries had their Christmas dinner last night. It was a lovely meal with all the trimmings except cranberry sauce.

After dinner, we went down to the girls' hostel where we had our Christmas tree fixed up with our presents. When I say Christmas tree, I do not mean one like you have at home. It was just a limb off a eucalyptus tree. Where leaves were missing, we tied some in to fill in the space.

Dr. Hynd brought someone dressed as Santa to the party, with the horn honking all the way. We all ran to the door to meet him, and Santa came limping in on a cane. Marilyn was so scared she was shaking. She finally got up the courage to speak to him.

At noon on Christmas Day, we were all invited to eat with the Africans on the station. They put up a big arbor near the church. We had meat and broth, hominy, pumpkin greens, tea, and cookies.

This was the first time we attempted to teach our people to give instead of always receiving a gift. Everyone on the station tried to find a gift for a name drawn in the gift exchange. One got a tomato, another some onions, and even safety pins. There were some interesting gifts. Even a piece of soap was very acceptable.

Swamped with Work

Miss Cole, a nurse from Montana, had to leave last week. She went home to be with her father, who is very sick. So I am now also in charge of the men's ward. We have about 125 patients. I wish you could see that ward at night. It doesn't have nearly enough beds. We put the sickest patients in beds. Others that are recuperating, or in casts, are up and around during the day. They are outside during the day, but at night they all come in. Then mats are rolled out, between beds, under beds, and all around until one can hardly get around in the room.

Malaria is raging. Some days we admit 15 or more with high temperatures of 105 and 106 degrees. Dr. Hynd had to go to Johannesburg this past week, and there is no other doctor around here except the army doctor. He comes twice a day for an hour to see the worst patients. When I admitted a very sick patient with a fever of 105 degrees and asked him what to do, he would say, "Just carry on with the usual treatment." So I have been very much on my own.

One of the African nurses climbed the little ladder leading to the attic above the male ward to retrieve something we had stored up there. All of a sudden, she made a dusty debut through the ceiling. She had stepped off a rafter onto plasterboard, which would not support her weight, and landed on the foot of a patient's bed. It was fortunate that neither the patient nor the nurse was injured. It could have been a very serious accident had she landed on the cement floor, on the patient, or on the metal parts of the bed.

Hats Off to Miss Skinner

I have always had a lot of sympathy for Miss Skinner, who is in charge of the laundry. She has no modern conveniences to work with. While she has plenty of African help, that does not help on rainy days. I don't know how she has kept our big hospital running with its constant need for clean linen. Clothes have to be hung out on long lines at the back of the hospital. When it rains, she has no place to dry the linens, and sometimes the shelves are empty and linens are badly needed. When a parcel arrives with sheets or bandages, she is delighted.

Miss Skinner and her helpers mending laundry for the hospital at Bremersdorp.

One of our men, who is crippled, helps her with the mending. Sheets that are worn in the center are torn down the middle and then the outer edges are sewn together. When they are no longer usable that way, she tears them up into bandages. Nothing ever goes to waste. Don't ever think that the time you sat and rolled bandages there in the States was time wasted. Everything you send is a very precious commodity to us here.

Missionary Meeting

Next week we have our annual district meeting with the women. We are also having the children at the same time. I am expecting a big crowd this year, for I gave the children an all-day sucker last year. It was probably the first they had ever had. I am sure they will remember and bring others this time. Working with the children is enjoyable but is also frustrating because I so seldom have anything to work with to make it interesting for them.

Little Eric

Eric is a 12-year-old boy who has visited us at the hospital many times. Because of malaria, his spleen is very large. After each treatment he returns home, but before long he is back again. This is his fourth time to be admitted for treatment.

Last Christmas Day, at the church, he gave himself to the Lord. Not many days later, his abdomen began filling with fluid again. The doctor would aspirate it, but in another day or two the procedure would have to be repeated. There was very little hope for him. We knew he could not live much longer in that condition. His mother, who had seen him suffer so much, begged the doctor to operate and remove Eric's spleen. The doctor hesitated. Because the boy was so ill, he was afraid Eric would not come through the surgery. The mother insisted, for she knew her child would soon die without the surgery.

So early the next morning we gathered together in the operating room with sad hearts and prepared to operate. The doctor first gave him a spinal, but because of the length of the operation, he finally had to give ether. Before the ether took effect, and while Eric was still conscious and the doctor was operating, Eric looked up into our faces. With a smile, he told us how happy he had been since Jesus had saved him. Then he began singing Zulu choruses that he knew. He asked one of the nurses to sing, but she wasn't sure it was the time or place for her to sing. So, without hesitation, Eric began to sing, in English, "Since Jesus Came into My Heart." That was more than just a chorus to him. That was his testimony, and we could see it reflected on his face.

After two and one-half hours of surgery, Eric was taken to his room. His condition was quite good. His spleen weighed three pounds, 11 ounces, about seven times what a normal spleen should weigh.

He made remarkable progress, and after a time of recuperation, he was out in the yard playing with the other recuperating children.

Dr. Hynd with Eric following his recuperation from surgery.

This week the doctor had to make a trip to the country. Since he had to pass Eric's house, he took Eric along. His mother was out in the garden plowing. When she heard that Eric was home, she ran to the house to see if her child was really well, or if they were bringing a corpse home to her. Eric's mother was so happy when she saw her child, and when the doctor came back by their home, the mother was out at the road to thank him. Eric is happy now, too, for he is free from pain.

Prayer and Fasting Day

Today is Prayer and Fasting Day. It is a time when we all

try to get in one-half hour of prayer sometime during the day and fast our noon meal. When I left to go on duty this morning, I promised Elmer that I would be home at 10:30 for a cup of tea, for we knew we would have no noon meal. Come and go with me through the day.

Upon arrival at the hospital I learned that two of my patients that I had admitted the night before had pneumonia. Two of my bed patients had been moved to the floor so that the pneumonia patients could have beds. I went to the ward where I found the nurses finishing up the morning baths. One nurse looked especially distressed. I found she was frustrated over the lack of clean linens. It had rained for two days, and the sheets did not get dry. I frantically searched the linen room and came up with some old blankets that she could use.

While helping with the linen, I heard a funny noise coming from the patient in the opposite corner of the room. I ran over to see what the trouble was. The man had a serious head injury received in a beer drink fight. To my horror, the man was having trouble breathing and looked like he would die at any minute. I quickly sent for the doctor, but by the time he could get there the man had stopped breathing. We worked with him for some time, but in spite of all we could do, he died.

After this, the doctor said he was ready to make rounds. I got my little order book and away we went. For the next several hours we saw and treated patients—ones with pneumonia, several with malaria, some with head wounds from fights, one with typhoid fever, and one child that needed a cast on his leg.

While I was preparing some of the injections and treatments, one of the nurses came to me and said, "Mrs. Schmelzenbach, I'm just sick. I just delivered a baby, and I think it is an albino." I went with the nurse to the maternity ward to talk with the mother. She was heartbroken. She is a Christian and this will be a real test for her and her husband.

The doctor and I went to the outpatient clinic to see several patients. One was a man who tried to get the doctor to say that he was blind so that he wouldn't have to pay any taxes; another was a man who had been sent to us for psychological testing to ascertain his mental abilities. I wrote two prescriptions for European patients, went to the antenatal clinic to check on a baby, and made one last round of the ward to make sure everything was going well before I went off duty. Just as I was leaving, I heard groans from the African nurses. They had been sent for by the doctor to attend an anatomy class where the doctor was performing an autopsy he wanted them to observe. I offered to stay in the ward so that they could all go. As I sat down to write the day's report, one of the nurses came with the news that a little boy had just been brought in with a large gash on his leg. By the time I had put a couple of stitches in his leg, the nurses were back from anatomy class and at last I could go home.

It was now 5 P.M.—Prayer and Fasting Day. I knew I had certainly fasted, but I hadn't had too much time to pray. I was sure the Lord knew my heart and understood.

Home at last—tired but happy to be with my family. I thought of all the letters I should have written today. Perhaps tomorrow I can do that, but tonight I am tired and it is early to bed for me.

Camp in the Bushveldt

The preachers have been asking for a camp for some time to which they could bring their families. They wanted to make a special effort to win their own children first before going after others. So, last Monday, Elmer, some national worker, and I went about 40 miles down in the bushveldt to hold a camp. We took enough provisions for 28 missionaries, their children, and over 200 Africans.

We went early to set up the camp. Brush had to be cleared, and framework for nine huge army sails had to be set up. These would be used for tents. We had a busload of frames and provisions to take. Then, when we arrived, it had to be taken off the bus and hauled about a mile into the bush by oxen on a very primitive road. We had an excellent camp, and we feel much good was accomplished.

After the camp, we took a little rest in Johannesburg. Now we are home again and are facing a new challenge.

5

A New Challenge

(1942-72)

Acornhoek, Eastern Transvaal

Council meeting is over, and we have been asked to go to Acornhoek in the Transvaal. Acornhoek is in the Republic of South Africa. Elmer felt a little reticent to leave Swaziland, as this is his home. We are wondering what the new area will do to my health. I know our house will have a grass roof and this could worsen my asthma, but we are willing to try if this is what the council wants. It will soon be moving day. I will write you when we are settled.

Acornhoek

We are now moved and face the challenge of working with over 1 million people who speak four different languages.

I will be in charge of the clinic while Miss Carpenter is away on a three-month holiday. This week I will also have my first clinic out in the bush. I am thrilled over that. We find that we like it here and are excited about the challenges we face.

We are not far from the Drakensberg mountains, and they are beautiful. Each evening we glory in a beautiful sunset.

I am in the process of registering our clinic with the government. When that is completed, they will then subsidize the patients and help with the cost of medicines.

Elmer at border station at Acornhoek

Yesterday I had my first clinic in the bush. I saw 47 patients. They have no means of getting help when they are sick, and it is too far for them to walk to the clinic.

A Birthday Party

Last Friday was my birthday. Mrs. Mischke fixed up a lovely lunch of sandwiches, pickles, deviled eggs, salad, ice cream, and a great, big birthday cake. When I thanked her, she said, "Well, if we didn't do it for each other, we would forget how."

Harmon Goes to School in Johannesburg

Our new station is 75 miles from the nearest school for Harmon. The Esselstyns have graciously offered to take Harmon in to live with them so he can go to school in Johannesburg. We are so grateful, but do not look forward to the time when he will have to leave.

* * *

Today was the day for Harmon to leave. Elmer took him to Nelspruit to meet Mr. Esselstyn who will take him back to Johannesburg. It is surely hard to send him off when he is only seven years old. It will be five months before school is out. To me, the only really hard sacrifice we missionaries make is sending our children away to school.

Clinic Work

We now have three clinics, and I see about 50 people in each. We had 16 inpatients and 500 outpatients last month. I now have the clinic registered as a hospital. The district doctor visits here once a week. That is a big help. We have had a telephone put in the clinic and have piped water from three 2,000-gallon tanks into the clinic.

Home Improvements

We are building a large bedroom on our house. I find that I cannot take the thatched roof any longer. The other missionaries call our new bedroom the European Ward. Someone else has been sick in it ever since we got it completed.

Our new bedroom windows are so near the path the children take going to school that we had to change the path immediately. There were just too many little faces at the glass wanting to see what was inside.

Shortly after the room was finished, we had a midnight serenade that really frightened us. Right outside our window a terrible noise erupted that lifted both Elmer and me straight up and out of bed. Standing there in the middle of the room, we wondered what on earth it could have been. We then realized that some donkeys were eating grass outside the house and the noise we heard was one of them braying near our open window.

The walls of our new room are made of mud brick. When they are dried they are covered with cement. The floor is cement, the ceiling is plasterboard, and the roof is corrugated iron. The only wood we used was for the door and the window frames. We got the wood from a sawmill 15 miles up in the mountains, and the plasterboard was brought from Nelspruit 75 miles away.

Famine Time Again

We are about to succumb to the heat. The people around us are hungry and thirsty. We have had almost no rain, and our water tanks and springs are all going dry. Some of the people walk 10 miles to get water at the rivers. All the crops are burned up.

Food is very scarce now. In many places there was no rain for the corn. People often walk half a day to a store to buy cornmeal. They can only get enough for one day, so the next day the process is repeated. It is a wonder they live.

Beginning next week the government will pay us for food for the children in school. We will be cooking a noon meal for them. They come to school early in the morning before they have anything to eat and don't get anything at home until late in the afternoon or early evening. Today we gave them porridge with soup over it made from tomatoes and onions. Tomorrow we will cook lettuce with ground-up peanuts. We will serve it over cornmeal porridge.

Our preacher has to walk nearly all day to get water and try to get home before dark. Recently, his wife went to get the water. She left home about 3 A.M. and returned around 1 P.M. She carried a large pot of water on her head. When she came into the yard, she stumbled and fell. She dropped the clay pot. It broke and she lost all the water. She just sat down and cried.

Her husband took a tin container and started out on the run to get more water. He ran almost all the way to the watering place. He had to wait until the lions left before he could get to the water. He also ran most of the way home and got there just in time for the children to have some water and cornmeal porridge before they went to sleep. It was the only food they had eaten all day long.

A Difficult Month

Harmon came home from school last Thursday for a month's winter holiday. On Saturday he came down with the measles. He has been very sick with a temperature of 105 degrees and bronchitis. He is some better now. Of course Marilyn was the next to come down with them.

The first two weeks Harmon was sick, the next two weeks Marilyn was sick, and now I am in bed. Tuesday was the doctor's day to be here, and I guess I worked too hard. Wednesday I had a miscarriage. It was a little boy about four months. Only a nurse from another station was here to take care of me. I'll be up in a few days and back to work.

Last Sunday we found a woman wandering down the road with cerebral malaria. Wednesday I was called out for a delivery. They didn't like the way I fixed up the baby, so they tried their medicine after I had gone. They got the baby's cord to bleeding. I was almost home when they came running and asked me to come back. I thought surely the baby would die, for it had lost so much blood, but it lived. I was called to another kraal to see a little girl about 12 years old. She had malaria.

A few days later a woman came to the clinic wanting me to pull a tooth. When I got the instruments ready, the demons took possession of her and she stiffened out and began to scream. We carried her out under a tree and left her alone. That seemed to quiet the demons. They like a lot of attention. I did not have to pull her tooth, for it was only a shell. She said that demons lived in it. I had two encounters with demons today. This has been some month!

M.M.M.

Do you know what that stands for? Men's Missionary Meeting. Today Elmer has gone to Johannesburg to have a missionary meeting with the men in the mines. There is quite a bit of rivalry between the men's and women's groups to see who can raise the most money. The women call themselves "the trains," for they feel they are strong and keep on going. The men call themselves “the elephants,” for the elephant comes along when the train is stuck and pushes it out. They have given Elmer the name of Missionary Elephant because he started the M.M.M.

Off to America

It has been nine years since we first came to Africa. Now, at last, we are going on furlough. Paul, Elmer’s younger brother, and his wife, Mary Kate, have just arrived here. They will take over our work while we are away.

I am writing this from Johannesburg where we have come to do some shopping and get ready to leave. During the day, we are trying to clear up all the red tape. Everything we take home has to be censored or have a permit. We have finished most of it. In the evenings Elmer goes with Mr. Esselstyn to the compounds to preach to our men in the mines.

* * *

We are in Argentina. We were booked to fly out of Buenos Aires but were held up for no apparent reason. Before we were finally able to leave, we had been in Argentina for six weeks. Many people were being detained. Some were even told to go back to Africa. We were told that we would have to have all our shots over again in spite of just having had them before we left Johannesburg.

We were concerned about the great expense of keeping our family in a hotel, so we called missionaries working in the city to see if they had a spare room. Mrs. Cochran, our missionary there, told us they had one bedroom but would be unable to cook for us since she would be away at Bible school. Mr. Cochran was touring the district.

Our stay in Argentina was a long, cold six weeks. Because we had left Africa during the heat of the summer, and we expected to arrive in America in hot weather, we had brought only lightweight clothes with us. So, we were uncomfortable and cold while we were in Buenos Aires. How happy we were to finally be on our way again.

Flying over the Amazon was a sight I will never forget. The river was so large, it seemed to me we were flying over water for several hours. It was my first experience on a large plane, and I prayed that the Lord would not let anything happen to the plane there. I just knew that rescuers would never be able to find us in all that water.

When we landed in Georgetown, British Guiana, Elmer and Harmon were taken to one army barracks, and Marilyn and I to another one to sleep the first night. I was apprehensive about being separated, but there was nothing I could do about it. The Lord was with each of us, and everything was all right.

We went on to Port of Spain and then Port-au-Prince where we were all lined up against a wall at the airport and had our temperatures taken. I have no idea what that was all about. From the airport we were taken to a hotel where food was served late, and then we were taken to our room.

At midnight I became violently ill. I had eaten some shrimp at dinner and did not know I was allergic to it. About 2 A.M. we were awakened and called back to the airport so that we could get an early flight to America. I was still feeling sick, but with Elmer's strong support, I made it. I vowed no more shrimp for me.

When we landed in Miami, Fla., and saw the American flag flying over the airport, our emotions almost got the best of us. Tears filled our eyes and big lumps came into our throats. It had been 9 years since we had seen our country's flag flying and 10 years since we had seen our folks. Our parents had never seen our children. How good it was to be home. The war years had kept us separated for so long.

The same day we arrived, after a little rest, we were taken to prayer meeting. We flubbed badly trying to speak English to Americans. The children were asked to speak, and they simply repeated some things Elmer had said.

A little later, back at the hotel, we found Harmon and Marilyn sitting in the middle of the big bed counting their missionary offering. They had stolen the show and had come back to the hotel with their hands full of nickels and dimes. They thought America was a wonderful place.

We traveled on to Kansas City to our church Headquarters. The train we were on was filled with soldiers. Many of them were sleeping in the train aisle with their duffle bags as pillows. We had to hold Harmon and Marilyn, then nine and six years old, on our laps. Upon our arrival, we reported in at Headquarters. They took one look at us and sent us off to a hotel to sleep, with instructions to report back the next day. Thus began our first furlough year.

Thanksgiving at Home

What could be nicer for a missionary than to be home with one's family for Thanksgiving? After nearly 10 years in a land far from loved ones, during a war and rationing, to be with family was an especially precious time.

We were excited to have many of my family together for that day. When it was time for dinner, it seemed the procession of food that kept coming with arriving family guests would never end. Finally it was time to sit down and eat. After a prayer of thanksgiving, we began to fill our plates. Floods of memories swept over me as I remembered those we had left in Africa who would have so little that day. I tried to eat, but there was a big lump in my throat, and I could hardly swallow. Tears came to my eyes, which I tried to hide from my family. After a bit, I was able to gain control of my emotions and enjoy the food and everyone present.

At breakfast, yesterday morning, Harmon pulled a garter snake from his pocket. Everyone scattered. When he was scolded, he said, "Well, it's a holiday and no one was at home to feed it so I brought it along." Needless to say, the snake was exiled to the garage at once. We had too many memories of poisonous snakes to live with one, even though it was harmless.

Our year in the United States was an interesting time with two youngsters unacquainted with so many new things.

Deputation—a New Adventure

Deputation is often difficult for both adults and children. Sometimes the children and I traveled with Elmer, but most often the children and I stayed home. Those were the days when missionaries and evangelists were entertained in the homes of the church people. We loved meeting the people, but after a few months of traveling by car and trying to keep the children entertained, we were very weary. Naturally, the people wanted to talk about Africa and ask questions. So it was often very late before we went to bed. Often we had to get up early because of the many miles between our two meetings. Sometimes our next meeting was only a few miles away. On those days, we would try to find a nice place to park the car. Elmer would read while I would try to entertain Harmon and Marilyn. However, the inconveniences were offset by the opportunity to make wonderful new friends. Some of these friends have become very close to us and have stood by us for years because of those times together.

Strange things often happen on furloughs. One of those experiences came about in Baltimore. When Elmer finished speaking he sat down on the platform on a little folding chair. When the district superintendent got up to speak, the chair Elmer was sitting on folded up completely and Elmer landed on the floor between the piano and an accordion player. Everyone tried not to laugh. I don't think anyone heard a thing the district superintendent said as they watched Elmer get up from the floor.

In spite of some of the crazy things that happened during that year of furlough, it was a good time and we had a change from the heat, drought, war, and rationing. But we were glad to be reunited again as a family full-time and return to Africa when the furlough came to an end.

Return to Africa

The years of war had made it impossible to send recruits to the mission field when they were needed. So, on our return, we were asked by the World Mission Department to take a party of 21 missionaries back to the field with us. Elmer and Rev. Robert Jackson were to be in charge. The trip was eventful enough to be a book in itself.

We were the first ones to fly out. Our first stop was to be Gander, Newfoundland, where we were to have breakfast. The place was so fogged in that we could not land, so we flew on to England. By the time we arrived, we were very hungry and tired since we had been up all night. When we landed in England, we were not allowed to leave the enclosed portion of the airport. They did serve us tea and tiny sandwiches.

When we stopped at Roberts Field Army Camp, we discovered one of the ladies had the mumps. The army doctor was anxious to get us out of there, so he told us her glands were swollen.

We landed later at Leopoldville, in the Belgian Congo, where we were to transfer to another plane. Although all arrangements had been made previously, there was no plane waiting. One hotel could not accommodate all of us, so the ladies and children were left in the hotel lobby while the men went to hunt other rooms.

The following day, when we got to the airport, we were told that the plane had left without us. Elmer argued with the clerk that the plane was secured, chartered for our flight only. We told the agency that any hold-up expenses would be charged to them as they had broken the contract. When they realized that we meant what we said, they did not keep us too long before they secured another plane for us that would land in Elizabethville.

This was to be a one-day flight, but the plane carried no food. Elmer knew everyone would be hungry, so he told the hotel cook to make us lots of sandwiches and provide us with two bananas each. The cook replied that they did not know how to make sandwiches. Elmer showed the cook what to do. He asked the cook not to put any meat in the sandwiches because it might spoil and make everyone sick.

Elmer went to a nearby bakery and bought cupcakes for everyone.

That afternoon we waited and waited for the cook and his helpers to bring the sandwiches and bananas. Finally everyone except Elmer went to bed. At ten o'clock that night there was a knock on our door. When Elmer opened it, there stood three men, each with a huge tray on his head, with the food we had ordered. Imagine our dilemma when we discovered that the sandwiches were actually small loaves of bread. We couldn't refuse them as the people had no use for sandwiches. Another problem was that they were handed to Elmer on huge trays, and nothing was wrapped. We asked for a box to carry the bread in, but there didn't seem to be anything available. How could we carry all this food with nothing to carry it in? Finally, I unpacked Marilyn's suitcase and we put the bread in her suitcase and jammed her clothes in other suitcases.

Early the next morning, we got on the plane. Mr. Jackson and Elmer were placed on opposite sides of the plane because of their weight. I wish you could have seen that plane. It looked as if it should have been junked a long time ago. When we were ready to take off, they wired the rear door shut.

Midmorning the plane landed in an isolated spot where there was a little food stand and several Catholic sisters. They offered us wine and fresh pork that had only been cooked a short time. No one ate or drank anything. We got back on the plane. How glad we were for the "sandwiches" and bananas we had brought.

The plane flew so low that we could clearly see the people walking along the pathways.

Marilyn went to the back of the plane where she found one of the little boys undoing the wire that secured the rear door. Mr. Jackson was sitting nearby. He grabbed the child and said, "I think your mother is calling you."

We had made arrangements for a train car to be waiting for us when we got to Elizabethville, but it was the same story over again. There was no car. Elmer and Bob Jackson told the clerk that our car was supposed to be there and since it was not, all the expenses we incurred in that town would be charged to them since they had broken the contract.

In the meantime, Elmer and Bob Jackson went out to the railroad yard nearby where they saw train cars standing. There was our car—the one we had contracted for. They kept us a few days longer, but at last we boarded the train for the last leg of our journey to Johannesburg.

We were glad to be on our way at last, but we weren't finished with our problems. We discovered there was not enough water on the train for all of us. Then we discovered there was no meal ticket for Marilyn. On top of this, the train crawled along so slowly and it was so hot that we weren't sure we would make it without someone getting sick. With everything wide open, one of the children dropped a toy out of a window. Rev. Meek jumped off the train, ran back, picked up the toy, and then caught the train again. That should tell you how slowly the train was going. It took us five days to get to Johannesburg. How glad we were to arrive!

Home Again

We are now back home at the same station we left—Acornhoek. It is good to get unpacked and settle down to a routine. We miss our loved ones in the States but know we are where God wants us.

Last Friday we made a trip to Nelspruit in the truck. We took a number of people with us. The King and Queen of England, with the two Princesses, Elizabeth and Margaret, are visiting our country. This was a real treat for us.

One of the first things Elmer did when we arrived home was to take a truckload of preachers to a revival at an outstation. However, because of the rains they could not get through on the muddy roads. The truck was stuck six times for a delay of three hours. They finally got the truck out by lifting the wheels and putting branches and stones under them. They were all a muddy mess when they got back here.

Going to Nelspruit to see the Queen of England

A New Arrival

Four days ago, on April 5, we welcomed a new arrival to our home. We named him Dennis Ray. Harmon and Marilyn were home from school for the weekend, and it was hard for them to go back to school on Monday morning and leave our new baby.

On Monday morning, missionary friends took all the children back to school. When they arrived back at Acornhoek, we were surprised to see they had all the children still with them. The children had been sent home because the school was quarantined for three weeks because of polio. Harmon and Marilyn were delighted to be home at this special time.

An Exciting Answer to Prayer

A man with a boring machine has just been here. He drilled down 165 feet where we hit an underground river—3,000 gallons per hour. What a wonderful answer to prayer. It seems too good to be true after all these years of carrying water up from the spring, which is a half mile from the house. Water was so scarce that first we bathed with it, then either scrubbed the floor or watered plants with it. Now it is plentiful. *Thank You, Lord, for another answered prayer.*

A Midnight Visitor

Grandmother Schmelzenbach was living with us, when, one morning, she told us that a mouse had run across her bed in the night. After breakfast Elmer and I went in to see if we could find it. Instead of a mouse, there in the open window, on the inside of the screen, was a green mamba, a very deadly snake. Had Grandmother Schmelzenbach moved or tried to find her flashlight, the snake would surely have struck her. There is no antivenom yet for the green mamba. Again, God's care was evident in our lives.

Ferns Alive

Last Sunday, while dinner was cooking, I walked out on the veranda to look at my houseplants. Elmer had made me a long bench and I had placed some painted 10-gallon cans on it. I had planted ferns in the cans. As I walked along looking at my plants, and picking off dead leaves, something shot a long tongue out and hit one of the buttons on the front of my dress. To my surprise, I discovered it was a chameleon that one of the children had put in my plants for safekeeping. We have always had several small lizards in the house. They are harmless and help keep down the mosquitoes. I discovered Sunday just how long a chameleon's tongue really is. The incident frightened me badly until I knew it was not a snake at the other end of that tongue.

Used Clothing

You will never know how much we have appreciated the clothing you have sent us for the national workers and their families.

Elmer fixed up one of the rooms in our basement with several rows of bars hanging from the rafters. As the parcels came, we opened them and sorted the clothes by size and hung them all on hangers on the bars. Twice a year I have told the preachers and their wives to come in and pick out enough clothes to outfit their families. They have appreciated picking out their own things. It has really helped to tide them over in these difficult times.

Christmas 1951

We have been trying to work up a little Christmas spirit in spite of the heat. It takes some adjustment in one's thinking to plan for Christmas when it is so hot.

The first thing on the agenda is a party with the preachers and their families. They always enjoy this because we prepare a nice dinner for them and then try to give them a gift for the family. This might be a sack of groceries, a four-gallon tin of kerosene, or a sack of flour.

Next comes the party with the boarding students before school closes. This year we thought it would be nice to try to make Christmas for the students a little more like our Christmas in the States. Also, since they are often on the receiving end, we thought it was time to teach them to give gifts as well. So, weeks before the party, they began trying to think of something they could give for the name they had drawn.

Party night came. The dining room in the girls' hostel was decorated, and we had a nice Christmas tree. The gifts were placed under it. When we returned from furlough, we brought a Santa Claus suit back with us. During the party, Elmer slipped out and put on the suit. Later he appeared in the doorway. Pandemonium broke loose. Students went out windows and doors. Those who couldn't get out went under tables. They had never seen anyone dress up as Santa. Before we could get the girls back into the room, Elmer had to take off the suit.

It was interesting to see the gifts they had brought for each other. There was a bar of soap, some safety pins, an orange, a piece of sugar, etc. They seemed to enjoy the gift exchange immensely. We worked the gift giving in with the Christmas story, and they understood why gift giving was a part of Christmas. After that, gift giving became a part of their Christmas tradition.

Busy Times

At the end of the month, there will be a farewell party for the boarding students before they go home. There will also be a farewell for one of the single ladies before she furloughs. Missionaries Herman and Mary Spencer will soon arrive, and we will plan a welcome for them. Then it will be time for a program in the church. This week, we also have a wedding in our home, and I will make the wedding cake. This couple are new Christians and want a Christian ceremony.

Christmas Day all the missionaries will get together and have dinner in the evening. It is too hot during the day and no one feels like eating. We will all bring something and put it together to make a nice Christmas dinner.

An Embarrassing Lesson Learned

At graduation time, we had a party for the junior high graduates. It was held in the boys' hostel dining room. We had fixed a nice chicken dinner for them. After dinner, we asked several boys to move the tables to the side of the room so that we could play some games. To our amazement, we discovered that as they ate their chicken, they had quietly dropped the bones under the table at their feet. When the tables were moved, there was a row of bones down the center of the room. The students were very embarrassed as they had to sweep the scraps out before they could play games. When one stops to think that the people are accustomed to eating outside around the campfire and throwing their bones to the dogs, then it is not difficult to understand why bones were thrown under the table.

We Entertain Company from Kansas City

Dr. Hardy Powers and Dr. Remis Rehfeldt have been here with us. They came out to accept the International Holiness Mission into the Church of the Nazarene. We had a big convention with over 200 people here for five days. All the people here worked very hard to make everything as nice as possible.

Our biggest worry was how to keep the meat from spoiling with the temperature at 100 degrees and more. Elmer made two big boxes, one a bit smaller. The smaller one fit inside the larger box. Between the two boxes we packed sawdust and dry ice.

All the provisions had to be brought here to the mission station from Nelspruit, 75 miles away. We put the meat—one cow, one hog, and some mutton—into the inner box and hoped we could keep it from spoiling with the dry ice.

We rented a refrigerator as we knew that three family-sized refrigerators could not cope with 200 thirsty people on hot days.

We made muslin bags and went up in the mountains and filled the bags with pine needles for mattresses. Every room in each missionary's house was in use and some rooms were curtained off to form small spaces for sleeping. We had warned the folks that were coming from other stations that they would be living under camping conditions and to come prepared. Everyone was a good sport, and we had a blessed time of spiritual refreshing together.

It was very impressive when Dr. Powers hit the table with his gavel and declared the International Holiness Mission a part of the Church of the Nazarene. One of the most exciting things for me is that we will now have another hospital just six miles from us. That will help with the load at our dispensary here.

A Few Good Laughs

Miss Lorraine Schultz gave us a good laugh the other day. She went out on horseback to visit one of the schools in an outstation close by. In the evening, when we were all together again, she said, "Mr. Mischke, do you know what that horse did?"

Mr. Mischke said, "No, what did she do?"

Miss Schultz said, "She stood right there in the road and had an *ingane*." (The word means baby.) Elmer and Mr. Mischke had a good laugh before they could stop long enough to tell Lorraine that she should have used the word *incane,* which means stubborn spell.

One missionary gave a devotional and talked about the angels in heaven. After the service, one of the nationals came to her and told her that if the mosquitoes were so bad in heaven, he didn't think he wanted to go there. The missionary had used the word for mosquito instead of angel.

In a language that one is still trying to learn, it is very easy to use the wrong word. We really appreciate our African people who never laugh at our efforts in Zulu, at least not until they are amongst themselves.

Self-support—a Hard Lesson

We have been trying to teach our churches self-support. It is hard when they have so little money. We went to an outstation recently to hold a service. Elmer was doing his best to teach them that lesson. Finally, one of our oldest men, a preacher, asked Elmer if he could try to explain it to the people. He came to the platform and told this story:

"I had a very good friend who had a wonderful, big hunting dog. This dog had been trained well and was such a good hunter that he could keep the family in meat. But, as more and more people moved into the area, the animals went farther and farther away. One day, the man and his dog went three days away from home to hunt. They got so tired and hungry that the dog refused to go any farther. The man got frightened and wondered how he would get the dog home. He was too big to carry, and the man loved his dog too much to leave him. Finally, the man had a thought. He got out his machete and chopped off half of the dog's tail. The dog yelped, then laid down. The man took the portion of tail to the fire and roasted it nicely, salted it, and gave it to the dog to eat. The dog enjoyed it, and the next morning had the strength to go on.

"By nightfall the dog was famished again and refused to move on. Again, the man took his machete and cut off the rest of the dog's tail, roasted it, and gave it to the dog to eat.

The next morning the dog had enough new strength to travel another day. The man and his dog got home that night, and the dog did it on his own tail."

"Now," said the preacher, "if we want to be self-supporting and make our own way, we are going to have to do it on our own tails."

His listeners got the point, and we heard a lesson we have never forgotten.

A Close Call

Since our children have had to be away at boarding school from the time they were six years old, we have made it a practice, the last few years, to go and get them every two weeks and bring them home for the weekend. The roads have been improved enough so that we can do this. It also gives us a chance to shop for needed supplies.

Early one morning we started out with Dennis and some other missionary children in the car. On the way Dennis became carsick. Elmer pulled the car over to the side of the road as close to the edge of the hill as possible with two wheels in a ditch. He had hardly stopped our car when a car came speeding around the mountain curve on our side of the road. Had we not been stopped and pulled over, there would surely have been a head-on collision. The driver veered to his side of the road at the last minute. He stopped his car and apologized profusely. How we thanked the Lord for His protecting hand over us again. Someone at home in the States must have been praying for us.

Creepy-Crawlies

We went to Green Valley today where Elmer was to preach. The host pastor sat in the doorway at the back of the church to prevent children from running in and out during the service.

In the middle of the message, the pastor got up, took his knobkerry, which is a three-foot stick with a knob on the end, and started for the platform. He walked up the aisle hunched over so as not to attract too much attention. I wondered just what he was going to do. He walked up to the wall behind Elmer, raised his club, and killed a big tarantula spider just behind Elmer. Then he turned around and went back and sat down.

On another occasion, someone went up to the platform and brushed a scorpion off the speaker's collar, killed it, and then sat down. This adds a whole new meaning to the question, "Am I my brother's keeper?" I guess this is why we become as a family on the mission station. We live and share together and become very close to each other.

I've only seen bedbugs a few times in my life, and I surely didn't expect to see them in church. At an outstation where we had gone to hold a service, someone was kind enough to bring Elmer and me each a chair to sit on. The seats were simply thongs of cowskin laced back and forth. When we got down on our knees to pray, I noticed that each hole the thongs went through was filled with bedbugs. One of the hardest things I have ever had to do was to sit on that chair for the rest of the service and keep my mind on the sermon. Someone told me that bedbugs only come out at night, so maybe that was why I was not bitten. One missionary told me that she didn't know there were bedbugs in that unknown bundle she left at the altar when she answered the call to be a missionary.

Time to Say Good-bye

It is time for furlough again. We are looking forward to it, and yet I don't like to think about it, for we will be leaving both Harmon and Marilyn at Northwest Nazarene College. We have been criticized for leaving Marilyn, but we feel we would like both children to have the chance to learn more of our church. They have had nothing but the mission station here. When they are away at boarding school, they go to other churches on Sunday as we have no European church at the school. I have to say it again. If there was ever a sacrifice that missionaries face, it is to have your children away from you and not be able to bring them up in a Christian home. Then, you have to send them thousands of miles away from home, across the ocean and wonder each and every day how they are getting along.

1955 and Time to Return to Africa

This furlough has been much the same as others. However our return will be vastly different. Harmon is registered in the college and Marilyn in the high school. All our plans for leaving went fine until three days before we were to leave. I ended up in the hospital with gall bladder surgery. Elmer stayed with me until the surgery was over and he knew I was going to be all right. Then he took Dennis and flew to Casa Robles to say good-bye to his mother, who was living there in the missionary retirement home.

While Elmer and Dennis went to Chattanooga, Tenn., for one more appointment Elmer needed to keep, I stayed in the hospital for 10 days. On the day I left I was so medicated that I hardly realized I was saying good-bye to my children. As we took off from Nampa, the stewardess gave me a pillow and I went to sleep, not even waking when the plane made a stop in Salt Lake City en route to Chicago.

Early in the morning Dr. Seaman met me at the plane, took me to their home for a day of rest, and then put me on another plane in the evening. I started for Louisiana early the next morning. Elmer was there to meet me. A few more days of rest and we were off to Africa by boat.

First Stop—Trinidad

We sailed from New Orleans via Trinidad. The Millers, who had served with us in Africa and whom we knew well, were now ministering in Trinidad. They begged us to stop and see them. Since our boat would be in the harbor for three days, we decided it would be nice to get off the boat and see the island.

Instead of docking close to shore, the boat anchored out in the ocean several miles from land. When we learned that, we knew it was useless to try to go ashore. However, in the middle of the first night, we heard someone on deck calling our names. We looked out our cabin door and there stood Mr. Miller. "Come on," he urged, "we want to take you ashore." So we dressed and went out on deck.

What a surprise! I looked over the side of our boat and there was Mrs. Miller in a little motorboat away down there in the ocean. Since I was still recovering from my surgery, I was reluctant to climb down a little rope ladder that I saw on the side of the boat. But the Millers were urging us to come to their home. So a sailor went down first, accompanying six-year-old Dennis; Elmer went down next, and I followed.

We went to the Miller home, had breakfast, and then Elmer spoke to the Bible school students. We did some sightseeing. Later in the day, we discovered Dennis had an abscessed tooth that had to be pulled.

On the third day we were to have dinner with another missionary family. As we drove up to their home, Mr. Harmon met us in the yard, waving his arms and shouting, "Don't stop here. The captain is hunting for you all over the island. The boat finished loading early and is ready to go."

We rushed down to the dock and could see the black smoke rolling out of the smokestack. The barge had already gone out to the boat to deliver other passengers who had been on the island. We had to hire another barge to take us out to the boat. Although it was the dinner hour, all the passengers were lined up on deck to see if we would make it. The captain later told us that they wouldn't have left without us because they had given us incorrect information about the departure time.

As the barge approached our boat, I could see that this time there was no rope ladder to climb. The crew had lowered some steps against the side of the boat. Our barge pulled in close to the steps, but to my dismay, I discovered that the bottom step was at least six feet above the barge. Each time a wave lifted the barge, one of the crew would toss one of us up on the steps. I was terrified, but the Lord helped me and we all made it. But can you imagine what a state I was in? I was still weak from surgery and by now was also suffering badly with asthma.

I had not had any trouble with asthma in the States, so I had very little medication with me. The few tablets I had were soon gone. I suffered and we prayed. Finally the day came when we landed. I got a little relief from a doctor in Cape Town. He told me to get away from the coast as soon as possible.

Back in Africa

While on furlough, Elmer purchased a large tent to take with him out on the district. He could set it up wherever it seemed like a good place to start a church. The tent was quite a curiosity and never failed to attract a crowd.

A friend gave us a loudspeaker system and a few records that we could use. When we started a new church in Champagne, we loaded our truck with Bible students and the loudspeakers. We parked under a tree. We played one of the records and waited for the people to come. Bible students had been dropped off in the area on our way to invite people to church.

Bible school students prepared to minister

One of the records we played over the loudspeaker was "When the Saints Go Marching In." While it was playing, I went to get something from the truck. When I went around to the other side of the truck, there were about 30 little boys having a real hoedown to the music. I called Elmer and I wish you could have seen the expression on his face. It was the last time we used that record.

Patience Learned the Hard Way

Learning patience is hard for some of us on the mission field. We were having our house painted on the inside by some of our nationals. Their work was excellent, but it seemed to me to be taking too long. So, with only two doors and a small picture railing around the top of the wall left to be painted, I decided we should finish the job.

Elmer and Dennis each got a brush and cans of cream-colored paint and started on the doors. I took a brush and a can of green trim to finish the picture railing. I climbed up on the chrome breakfast table and started painting. Everything went fine until the leg of the table decided to give way. I slid off the table easily, but my elbow hit the floor hard and my can of green paint splashed out and came down all over me. It covered my hair, face, glasses, and my dress, to say nothing of the newly painted, cream-colored wall.

Elmer and Dennis came running to help me, but when they saw I wasn't hurt, they laughed and laughed. It was their first encounter with a real green-eyed monster. I could not see a thing.

Animals Can Be Dangerous

Recently, when Elmer was coming home from a meeting at one of the outstations, he hit something in the road with the car. He got out to see what it was and found an anteater as big as a hog. I had no idea they grew that big. The men dressed it out and had a nice feast the next day.

Animals are so thick we have to be very careful when driving. When they see a car coming, they try to get across the road ahead of the car. I think a giraffe is the most dangerous. It runs across the road, and as the driver of the car speeds up, thinking it's safe, the giraffe comes in contact with a telephone wire and decides to go back across to the other side. Its legs are knocked from under it, and their heavy body falls on the car. Often the people in the car are killed and the animal's neck is broken as it falls to the ground.

Our Compensation

Sunday was a hard day. We didn't get home from the morning service until 3:30 in the afternoon. We had a tent meeting, and it was unbearably hot in the tent. Then when the dust gets stirred up, I can hardly breathe because of my asthma. But our compensation was 30 seekers at the altar.

We asked the Lord for 300 souls this year on the district. We have just closed three outstation revivals. Eighty new converts were saved at one station, 35 at another, and 52 at the third. It looks like we will have to raise our goal. This is our compensation for any inconveniences, and we praise God for so many finding Christ.

An African Night

Anyone who has not had the chance to sit out at night under our beautiful African sky and eat supper around a campfire has missed something wonderful.

When our children were still at home, we planned evening cookouts. They loved it. Early in the season when the reeds reached a good height at the river, Elmer would build a large reed enclosure, circular in shape, with one doorway. We would take folding chairs, build a fire in a brick fireplace, and cook our supper outdoors. Each missionary family would bring whatever food they had on hand and we would eat together.

There was no danger from animals, for too many people had moved in around the mission and the animals had moved farther away.

To sit and listen to a perfectly quiet evening was most relaxing. In the days of the satellites, we would sometimes see two of them go over in one evening. There were no city lights or cars to disturb us with noise and lights. We could pick out the Southern Cross and other constellations in the night sky, listen to the animal sounds in the distance, and enjoy the beauty of God's nighttime world.

About ten o'clock each family would pack their things away, fold up their chairs, and prepare to go home. That was how the day would end on Saturday, and we would go back to our stations prepared for a full day's work on Sunday. Nothing can take that happy memory from me.

Early Monday morning our children, with their lunch boxes filled with cookies and goodies, were taken back to school. We did not have much to entertain our children with, but they will never forget the experience of fellowship under the African night sky.

An Unusual Sunday Service

Elmer's policy for running the outstations was to enlist every missionary available at the station and in the hospital to help with the services. He asked them to be responsible for a service each Sunday. They would load up their cars with any who could go along and each go to a different outstation.

One Sunday, one of the nurses took several from the hospital and went to her preaching point, which was new and still meeting under a tree.

After Sunday School, they took a little break before starting the worship service. During this time a little boy spotted a beehive up in a tree. He found a stick and poked it. The bees angrily swarmed out of the hive and attacked our missionary nurse, stinging her badly. She became unconscious. When she finally came to, she found herself at the witch doctor's hut where he was about ready to give her something to drink.

One of the young men who had come with her knew how to drive, so they rushed her to the hospital where a doctor treated her. She was very sick and swollen for several days. They removed 300 stingers from her body.

The Chiefs of Arthurseat

During our stay at Arthurseat, the government sent men around the country to find convenient places where they could call all the chiefs of the area together. The government held classes for the chiefs and taught them many things that would help them in caring for their people.

They asked permission to come to our station. So, during the school holiday, we let them use our girls' dormitory. There were health classes, information about clean drinking water and diseases, as well as lessons about crop rotation, fertilizing, and ideas on how to grow better crops for food. Elmer was permitted to have a Bible class with them each day. We got to know each chief well, and thus we were able to minister in practically every area with the consent of the local chief.

One government man who had been on our station to teach, and whom we met in an office years later in Johannesburg, told us Doris Brown requested a church site in the Northern Transvaal. The official told us he did not know Doris Brown, but, when he saw that the site was for the Church of the Nazarene, he gladly signed the papers that gave her the site. We also made many friends with the government men who helped us out in our work.

An Unusual Marble Game

Occasionally, a bag of marbles came in a box work parcel. This is what must have happened; otherwise, I do not know how these grade school children ever got marbles.

One morning, on her way to school, Rose Handloser came across two little boys playing marbles. When she heard the boys choose different names for each side, she was interested and stopped to listen. The names the boys chose were Schmelzenbach and Satan. Now she was really interested to see which side would win. When she told us about it later, she said, "It turned out OK. Schmelzenbach won!"

6

Good-bye

After we had a hospital at Acornhoek, I was relieved of much of my work in the dispensary. I was then able to help Elmer more with the work of the district and in the office. During the next few years, we were transferred to Johannesburg, and then to Pietersburg.

All this time my asthma continued to worsen. Medicines brought unexpected reactions and side effects until the doctor finally sent me to the hospital in Johannesburg.

One Saturday night, while in the hospital, I went into a coma. The doctors told my family that I would not live more than eight hours. But missionaries and Africans went to prayer, and by midmorning of the next day I came out of the coma. In a few days I was able to go home to Pietersburg, much to the surprise of the doctors.

When we returned home, Elmer took me to the doctor who had sent me to the hospital in Johannesburg. He was a kindly, Christian man. When he saw me, he commented, "We can't take any credit for this; only God can perform miracles. Give her some time to get back on her feet again, then you must take your wife to the United States. The climate and conditions here are against her. The stress of your work is probably also responsible."

Those were the darkest days I ever saw Elmer go through. To leave the country, the people, and the work he loved so much was hard for him to accept. But he said, "All right, Lord, You have given Mary back to me, and Your will is my will. There must be a reason."

We packed our belongings, said good-bye to missionaries and our beloved Africans, and returned to the United States.

We spent the first year in deputation work. It seemed we almost lived in our car as we traveled all over the country holding meetings. After our last deputation service in the east, we drove back to Kansas City to report that our work was finished. We were offered a small church, but Elmer did not feel he could pastor after spending so many years on the mission field.

We drove to Garnett, Kans., where our daughter lived. It was a very quiet trip. As we drove along, neither of us had much to say; but we had plenty to think about.

Lying on the car seat between us was Elmer's Day-By-Day book. I picked it up and looked at it. I said, "Elmer, do you know you have a meeting in two weeks, and we still have no place to live?"

He looked at me and said, "Well, if that is what I am supposed to do for now, I'll do it. Maybe I can help a pastor get a new glimpse of missions."

After that meeting, the calls for other meetings began to pour in, and soon Elmer was completely scheduled.

A few mornings after Elmer had returned to Garnett from his last meeting, he received a phone call from Rev. Talmadge Johnson of Oklahoma City. "Elmer, your deputation is finished. Where are you going to live?" asked Rev. Johnson. "We don't know," answered Elmer. "Come to Oklahoma City," said Talmadge, "and I'll help you find a place."

We drove to Oklahoma City. When we arrived, Rev. Johnson was waiting for us. He drove us all over the area. By evening we had spotted a house we liked and we bought it.

Elmer's Last Meetings

When Elmer started his first deputation services after we came home, he scheduled them from Wednesday through

Sunday. Soon he discovered that he was not physically able to hold to that schedule, so his meetings were Friday through Sunday. A visit to the doctor revealed that he needed surgery. The surgery revealed a malignancy.

After the surgery and recuperation, he was on the road again trying to build up his social security to a level sufficient for me to live on when he was gone. He traveled seven more years before the cancer struck again.

They said that more radiation was needed. He was suffering greatly by this time. The first 42 cobalt treatments had given him constant pain. He felt he couldn't face any more treatments, but the doctor scheduled him for more radiation to begin the following day.

The night before he was to begin more radiation, Elmer went to bed about five minutes before me. When I came into the bedroom, I discovered he was gone. God had called him home.

A few days before his death Elmer had said to me, "I'm ready to go. My suitcase is packed. I have not one regret in my life. I have done my best."

Looking over his carefully kept yearly schedules, I found that he had visited over 1,000 churches. I could only guess how many sermons he had preached. I know he was often in pain when he spoke, but he was happy knowing he was helping the cause of missions.

Thus ended 54 years of a wonderful missionary career, and our life together. Many times we have each said, "If it were possible, we would do it all over again."

Missions pays great dividends. Yet so many have not heard. Let's invest all we can—our time, our prayers, our resources, ourselves—to take the Good News to our world.

Elmer and Mary Schmelzenbach on return visit to Africa in 1978 with Sina and children. Sina had served as the Schmelzenbachs' faithful housegirl for several years.

This book has been read by:

Betty Hodgkinson